22.83

DATE DUE

APR 2 6 2002	
JUN 1 8 2002	
JUL 2 - 2002	
OCT 2 - 2002	
MAY 1 6 2003	
JUL 1 8 2003	
SEP 1 9 2005	
APR 9 - 2006	
JUL 1 5 2006	
MAY 2 4 2007	

DEMCO, INC. 38-2931

W9-AMT-186

FEB 2 2 1999

Trees and Plants
in the
Rain Forest

Saviour Pirotta

RAINTREE
STECK-VAUGHN
PUBLISHERS
The Steck-Vaughn Company

Austin, Texas

Deep in the
Rain Forest

PEOPLE in the Rain Forest
PREDATORS in the Rain Forest
RIVERS in the Rain Forest
TREES AND PLANTS in the Rain Forest

Cover picture: A hummingbird feeding off the flower of a ginger plant

Title page: People in Indonesia collecting the stems of rattan plants, to be sold for furniture

Contents page: The rafflesia plant is the largest and smelliest flower in the world. It smells like rotting meat to attract the flies that pollinate it.

Published by Raintree Steck-Vaughn Publishers,
an imprint of Steck-Vaughn Company

Printed in Italy. Bound in the United States.
1 2 3 4 5 6 7 8 9 0 03 02 01 00 99

Library of Congress Cataloging-in-Publication Data
Pirotta, Saviour.
Trees and plants in the rain forest / Saviour Pirotta.
    p.   cm.—(Deep in the rain forest)
    Includes bibliographical references and index.
    Summary: Describes the different types of trees and plants that grow in layers of the rain forest, the fruits, nuts, and vegetables they provide, and what threatens their survival.
    ISBN 0-8172-5134-0 (hard); 0-8172-8112-6 (soft)
    1. Rain forest plants—Juvenile literature.
    2. Rain forests—Juvenile literature.
    3. Rain forest ecology—Juvenile literature.
    4. Rain forest plants—Utilization—Juvenile literature.
    5. Forest products—Tropics—Juvenile literature.
    [1. Rain forest plants. 2. Rain forests. 3. Rain forest ecology. 4. Ecology.]
    I. Title. II. Series.
QK938.R34P57   1999
581.7'34—dc21   97-43891

Contents

Rain Forests Around the World

Rain forests are thick forests in parts of the world where there is lots of rain. Most of them are near the equator, an imaginary line that runs around the center of the earth. The biggest rain forest is the Amazon, in South America.

A rubber tapper collects sap from a rubber tree in India.

Cocoa pods ▶ are shelled in Indonesia.

EQUATOR

◀ The rafflesia flower is found only in Southeast Asia.

4

Rain forests have more types of trees and plants than exist anywhere else. Since rain forests are always hot and wet, trees and plants can grow in them all year round.

◀ Chicle resin is molded into cubes in Guatemala. Chicle is used to make chewing gum.

KEY
◼ The green areas on the map show rain forests.

▲ A vegetable harvest in Brazil.

▲ A ginger plant feeds a hummingbird in Costa Rica.

Rain Forest Layers

The rain forest has different layers, like a house with different floors. Different plants and animals live in each layer.

All the plants in the rain forest are especially suited to their own layer.

▼ A diagram showing three layers of the rain forest

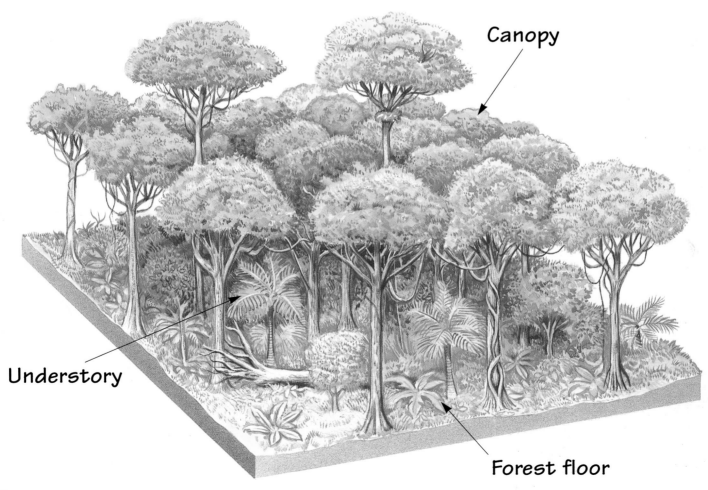

Canopy

Understory

Forest floor

The colorful toucan lives in ▶ the branches of the canopy.

The canopy

The top layer of the rain forest is called the canopy. It is made of the thick branches of trees tangled together.

◀ The three-toed sloth also lives in the canopy. It is very good at climbing trees.

▲ The fan palm tree has big leaves. They help catch sunlight underneath the canopy.

The understory

Under the canopy is the understory, where bushes and smaller trees grow. There is not much light in the understory, so trees and plants grow only where light shines through.

◄ When the fruits of the cannonball tree fall to the ground, they make a loud, booming sound.

Forest floor

At the bottom is the hot, dark forest floor. Fungi, ferns, and herbs grow there. They grow in a mixture of soil and dead leaves, which fall from the trees.

The forest floor is always crawling with insects and termites. Many are camouflaged to look like their surroundings.

▼ These leaf-cutter ants are carrying leaves that are twice their size.

Needing One Another

Trees, plants, and animals in the rain forest all need one another to grow. Flowering plants grow on the branches of trees high up in the canopy, where the sunshine can reach them.

▲ Two tree frogs in a pond made of leaves, up in the canopy.

The leaves of plants form little ponds for frogs, crabs, and insects to live in. Some plants feed off the bodies of dead insects. When the insects die, they become food for the plants.

▼ An orchid growing on a tree, high up in the canopy.

Food for animals

▲ A monkey eating fruit in the Amazon rain forest, in Brazil.

Fruit trees in the canopy provide food for animals. After the animals eat the fruit, the seeds in their droppings are left on the ground. The seeds in the fruit grow into new trees.

 12

Birds and bees

Birds and bees feed on nectar from flowers. Without knowing it, they repay the flowers by fertilizing them with pollen. The pollen sticks to their bodies as they feed on the nectar. When the birds and bees fly to the next flower, the pollen rubs off.

▼ A hummingbird feeding on the nectar of a ginger flower in Costa Rica.

Fruits of the Forest

The rain forest provides lots of food for people, as well as for animals. Many juicy fruits, like bananas, mangoes, pawpaws, and star fruit grow all year round.

Next time you visit a supermarket, look around for these rain forest fruits.

◀ This Kayapo boy in Brazil has collected a harvest of beans.

A girl in Indonesia splitting open the ▶ pods of cocoa fruit, to get to the fleshy nuts inside

Vegetables like manioc, sweet potatoes, and breadfruit are grown by farmers for their families to eat. Tea, coffee, cocoa, and cereals are grown to be sold to other countries.

Buriti palm tree

The buriti palm tree is very important to the people of the Amazon. It can be made into oil, wine, starch, cork, and fiber for making string. No wonder they call it the "Tree of Life!"

▼ A woman in New Guinea making palm oil from the fruit of the buriti palm tree

The fruit of a buriti palm ▶ tree in Brazil

Brazil nuts

Brazil nut trees grow wild in the Amazon. People collect the nuts in huge baskets and sell them in the markets.

Most Brazil nuts are sold to other countries. They are popular in countries like Great Britain and the United States, especially at Christmastime.

A girl in Peru with a ▶ harvest of Brazil nuts. The shells have been taken off the nuts.

Rubber and Chewing Gum

Thousands of families in the rain forest earn their living from one kind of tree—the rubber tree. They are called rubber tappers.

Rubber tappers make deep cuts in the tree trunk, which oozes a milky sap.

◀ A rubber tapper collecting sap from a rubber tree in India

Rubber tappers collect the sap in cups. Later, they mix it with water and acid, and it turns into solid rubber. Rubber tappers sell the rubber to factories in their own country and abroad.

▲ This man is heating rubber sap in a pan over a fire to dry it.

Chewing gum

Did you know that chewing gum comes from a tree in the rain forest, too? It is called the sapodilla tree. People collect its sap, called chicle, in the same way that rubber tree sap is collected. The sap is boiled until it is hard. Then it is sent to the chewing gum factory.

▼ Chicle is molded into cubes before it is sent to the chewing gum factory.

▼ A chicle tapper making deep cuts in a sapodilla tree to drain the chicle

Rattan

Thousands of people in Indonesia earn their living from rattan, which is a thorny, climbing plant. Rattan can grow up to 650 ft. (200 m) long.

The thicker stems are used to make furniture. Others are split into fine strands and made into baskets or rope. Most rattan furniture is sold to other countries.

▼ A woman splitting rattan cane into fine strands, to be woven into baskets

▼ Rattan collectors with hooped stems of rattan

The Forest in Danger

Rain forest people are very careful to take from the forest without harming it. But new arrivals are not so careful. Settlers from the city and large companies burn down vast areas of forest for farmland and mining.

Sad to say, the new farmland does not last long. The rain washes away the soil, and the land becomes a desert. Then the settlers and companies move on to burn more forest.

▲ It takes only ten years for rain forest that has been burned to turn into desert.

◀ Rain forest is burned by a large company, to clear the land for farming.

Logging

Logging companies cut down thousands of trees each year. They sell the wood to countries like the United States, to be made into furniture.

Without the trees, many plants, animals, and insects lose their homes and die. Many species become extinct every day.

▼ A logging company has just cut down these trees. It will sell them to be made into furniture.

▲ A logger beside a tree he has just cut down in Borneo.

No wonder rain forest people are fighting to save their land and trees. They know that farmers can grow crops without burning down the trees. They want loggers to cut down fewer trees, not whole areas of forest.

People in rich countries can help save the rain forests, too, by not buying things made of precious woods, like mahogany.

Rain Forest Ice Cream

Use ingredients that come from the rain forests to make this exotic, tutti frutti ice cream.

YOU WILL NEED:

FOR THE ICE CREAM

2 scoops of vanilla ice cream

1 banana and 1 mango, chopped and sliced

crushed Brazil nuts

a spoonful of cocoa

2 small chocolate candies

TO DECORATE THE GLASS:

drinking glass

rubber band

scissors

green paper, or paper colored with green crayons

an empty bottle

To make the ice cream:

1. Put the chopped fruit into the bottom of the glass.

2. Cover with two scoops of ice cream.

3. Sprinkle on the crushed nuts and cocoa, and top with the chocolate candies.

28

To decorate the glass:

1. Draw the leaf diagram above on green paper four times and cut the leaves out with scissors. Make the leaves taller than your glass.

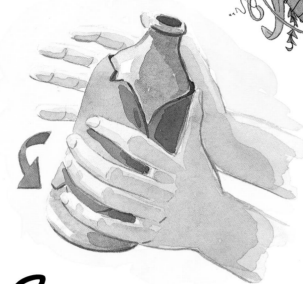

2. Wrap the leaves around the bottle to make them curl.

3. Secure the bottoms of the leaves around the glass with a rubber band.

4. Make sure the leaves curl outward, so the glass looks like a leaf pond in the canopy.

Glossary

Amazon A region of rain forest in South America around the Amazon River.

Camouflaged Disguised to look like the surroundings.

Canopy The roof of the rain forest, formed from the tangled branches of trees.

Crops Plants that are grown for food, including wheat, corn, and rice.

Fertilizing Making something able to reproduce.

Fungus A type of plant. Mushrooms and molds are fungi.

Manioc A root vegetable that grows under the ground and can be used in many different dishes.

Pollen The fertilizing powder in plants.

Rattan A plant that has long, thick stems, which are used to make baskets and furniture.

Settlers People who move to a new place to live.

Species A group of the same type of plant or animal.

Rubber tappers People who collect the sap of the rubber tree.

Further Information

Other books to read

Cherry, Lynne. *The Great Kapok Tree: A Tale of the Amazon Rain Forest.* San Diego: Harcourt, Brace, Jovanovich, 1990.

Grupper, Jonathon. *Destination—Rain Forest: Rain Forest.* Washington, DC: National Geographic, 1997.

Harris, Nicholas. *Into the Rainforest: One Book Makes Hundreds of Pictures of Rainforest Life* (The Ecosystems Xplorer). Alexandria, VA: Time Life, 1996.

Lewington, Anna. *Atlas of the Rain Forests.* Austin, TX: Raintree Steck-Vaughn, 1997.

Nagda, Ann Whitehead. *Canopy Crossing: A Story of an Atlantic Rainforest.* Norwalk, CT: Soundprints Digital Audio, 1997.

Osborne, Mary Pope. *Afternoon on the Amazon.* (First Stepping Stone Books). New York: Random House, 1995.

CD Rom

Exploring Land Habitats (Wayland, 1997)

Useful addresses

All these groups provide material on rain forests for schools:

Earth Living Foundation
P.O. Box 188
Hesperus, CO 81326
(970) 385-5500

Friends of the Earth
1025 Vermont Avenue NW
Suite 300
Washington, D.C. 20005-6303
(202) 783-7400

Reforest the Earth
2218 Blossomwood Court NW
Olympia, WA 98502

The World Rainforest Movement
Chapel Row
Chadlington
Oxfordshire OX7 3NA
Tel: 01608 676691

World Wildlife Fund
1250 24th Street NW

Picture acknowledgments
Bruce Coleman (Alain Compost) *Title page*, 23, (Gerald Cubitt) 4 (top right), 15, (Luiz Claudio Marigo) 16 (top), 19; Sue Cunningham Photographic Library 5 (top right), 14; Ecoscene (Wayne Lawler) 8 (top), 22; NHPA (Martin Harvey) 26 (middle); Oxford Scientific Films (Michael Fogden) *Cover*, 5 (top left), 13, (Harold Taylor) 8 (bottom), (J. A. L. Cooke) 10, (Tui De Roy) 11, (Jim Clare) 12; Edward Parker 26 and 27; Planet Earth Pictures (Georgette Douwma) *Contents page*, 4 (bottom), (Thomas Wiewandt) 7 (top); South American Pictures (Chris Sharp) 20, (Tony Morrison) 24 and 25; Still Pictures (Nigel Dickinson) 5 (bottom), 21, (Jany Sauvenet) 7 (bottom), (Norbert WU) 9, (Dominique Halleux) 16 (bottom), (Hellier Mason) 17, (Julio Etchart) 25; Wayland Picture Library (David Cumming) 4 (top left), 18.
Border and folio artwork: Kate Davenport. Map pages 4–5 and artwork page 6: Peter Bull

Index

Entries in **bold** show there is a picture on the page.